One Clear, Still Night

Thirty-One Advent Devotionals with Inspirational Readings, Recipes and Ideas to Help Make Christmas Meaningful

Wendy,
May you find special
meaning in this holiday
season.

Written by
Terri A. Groh

Terri

One Clear, Still Night

Thirty-One Advent Devotionals with Inspirational Readings, Recipes and Ideas to Help Make Christmas Meaningful

Written by Terri A. Groh

Email: terri.groh@aol.com
Website: www.terrigroh.com

Cover photo by Terri A. Groh

Scriptures taken from the Holy Bible, New International Version®, NIV®. Copyright © 1973, 1978, 1984, 2011 by Biblica, Inc.™ Used by permission of Zondervan. All rights reserved worldwide. **www.zondervan.com** The "NIV" and "New International Version" are trademarks registered in the United States Patent and Trademark Office by Biblica, Inc.™

ISBN-13: 978-1484801505

ACKNOWLEDGEMENTS

This book is dedicated to my mother, Dianne Empie. As a single mom she struggled to make ends meet. There was never enough money and life was hard. Yet, she always did her best to make Christmas a special time. She took us to church, even before she came to know the Lord. She sacrificed and scrimped and saved so her children would have a nice Christmas.

I love you, Mom, and I'm so thankful for you, and for helping to make Christmas meaningful to me.

INTRODUCTION

One clear, still night a miraculous event took place. All of creation held its breath in anticipation and then released it as a baby's wail pierced the darkness. The Savior of the World was born in a dark, dusty, dirty manger. The stars shone bright. Angels sang with praise and joy in the night sky.

This event has changed lives. Jesus birth, life, subsequent death and resurrection still have an impact on people today.

A Savior was born to bring hope and joy; to bring order to the chaos. He came to free those captured in the bonds of sin and despair.

One clear, still night Love was born.

As you read these words of encouragement, I pray that your life, too, will be changed by the One who brought hope into the world.

At Christmas we focus on the glitter and glamour and on the busyness and activity. Take time each day to stop, to listen, and to reflect on the true meaning of Christmas.

This book of Advent devotionals will help you do just that. Grab a cup of coffee and stop the running and just sit and hear from God. Gain new meaning from the Christmas story.

I have included some questions to ponder at the end of each devotional, as well as lines for you to journal your thoughts and ways the Lord is speaking to you.

Interspersed throughout the book are different inspirational readings, recipes and ideas to help make Christmas meaningful.

Christmas is special. It is a time to give gifts and celebrate. As you reflect on the symbolism and meaning of the Christmas story, I pray that your holiday will be made even more significant.

December 1

Not Good Enough

Luke 2:8-12 ~

And there were shepherds living out in the field nearby, keeping watch over their flocks at night. An angel of the Lord appeared to them, and the glory of the Lord shone around them, and they were terrified. But the angel said to them, "Do not be afraid. I bring you good news of great joy that will be for all the people. Today in the town of David a Savior has been born to you; he is Christ the Lord. This will be a sign to you: you will find the baby wrapped in cloths and lying in a manger.

"I am not good enough." "I don't measure up." "I am insignificant." Have you ever felt this way?

When I was in high school I dated a young man who came from a wealthy family. He had the best of everything. Anything he wanted, he received. I, on the other hand, came from a family who struggled to make ends meet. My mother, a single parent, worked long and hard hours just to stay afloat.

This boy's family had a huge home, race horses, and the newest car. I had hand-me-downs, lived in an apartment, and had access to the family car once in a great while. Over time, it became apparent that he felt like he could do better than me. I never felt good enough and that hurt.

The angel that appeared to the shepherds on that clear, still night told them that the good news was for all the people. There was no discrimination. No one was insignificant. All were important.

The shepherds were a group of rough and rugged men who were not the cream of society. The good news the angel shared wasn't just for the wealthy or the Jews; it was for everyone – poor, outcast, rich, Jews and Gentiles. It was also intended for those shabby shepherds.

Look at the genealogy of Jesus listed in Matthew, chapter one, and you will find a very interesting family tree. His ancestry is comprised of a deceiver, a Gentile, a prostitute, a murderer, an adulterer, a king, a rich man, and a poor girl to name a few. It is wonderful to realize that the Savior has a family tree that is representative of the type of people He came to save.

As you go through this Christmas season take some time to reflect on the wonderful gift that the world received that Christmas long ago. Remember that Jesus came into this world to save all men and women, no matter what they have done or where they come from.

Your genealogy does not matter. Your social position is not important. Your accumulation of earthly possessions is meaningless. Jesus came for you regardless of your status.

Isn't that wonderful news?

Spend some time in prayer, thanking God for your significance in Him.

_____

_____

_____

_____

_____

_____

_____

_____

_____

_____

_____

_____

_____

December 2
Joy Comes in the Morning

Psalm 30:4-5 ~

Sing to the Lord, you saints of his; praise his holy name. For his anger lasts only a moment, but his favor lasts a lifetime; weeping may remain for a night, but rejoicing comes in the morning.

Luke 2:9-11 ~

An angel of the Lord appeared to them, and the glory of the Lord shone around them, and they were terrified. But the angel said to them, "Do not be afraid. I bring you good news that will cause great joy for all the people. Today in the town of David a Savior has been born to you; he is the Messiah, the Lord.

Things always seem darkest before dawn and so bleak in the dead of the night. In the darkness I am alone with my thoughts. Many a night, I lie awake mulling over the events of the day. I begin to feel conviction about how I handled a situation or remorse over some sinful behavior or attitude I exhibited.

7

This is the time I'll begin to think about a problem or my anxieties will flare-up over a situation I am facing. As I toss and turn, trying to get back to sleep, all the fears and concerns keep bubbling up to the surface.

However, I also find that with the morning light things always seem better. I find my spirits lifted and I'm ready to face the new day. The things that seemed so frightening to me in the middle of the night are chased away by the dawning of a new day. I have renewed hope.

The Israelites were in a long night of darkness and depression. They were longing for a Savior. After hundreds of years of hoping and waiting for the Messiah things seemed bleak. Then one unexpected night God showed His favor and a baby was born.

Joy! Excitement! Spirits renewed! Morning had dawned for the nation of Israel. Hope and great joy had come to them. Finally, after the long night of waiting, wrestling and longing, God sent them the Savior for whom they had waited.

This holiday make a conscious effort to remember why you have hope and joy. Don't forget why you can greet each new day with renewed excitement and encouragement. That hope is because God came and dwelt among the people He loved.

Remember what He has done in your life and feel His joy and renewed hope this morning.

What has God done in your life that brings you joy? Make a list of those things and spend some time focusing on them.

_____

_____

_____

_____

_____

_____

Christmas Traditions

Christmas is the time of year that I look forward to with great anticipation. I love every single thing about it. The sights, the smells, and the sounds are meaningful to me. Over the years we have developed a few traditions that our whole family loves.

I am sharing these, not so you will copy them exactly, but to get you thinking about some traditions you have or can begin to implement in your own home.

1. Ornaments. Each year we purchase an ornament for the children and I put their name and date on it. We love unpacking them each year, and reminiscing over the past Christmases. We hang them on the tree for all to enjoy. I will keep them until the children set up homes of their own, and then they will receive them to use on their own Christmas tree.

2. Jesse Tree. When our children were younger, we did this every year. There is much information that you can find online about the Jesse Tree. It is a symbolic way to trace the genealogy of Jesus from creation to the birth of Christ. We would sit and read a daily devotional together and then hang an ornament on our table top Jesse Tree. It was a wonderful way to celebrate advent.

3. Tree trimming day. The day after Thanksgiving we pull out all the Christmas decorations and decorate the tree together as a family. I make Christmas cookies and hot cocoa and we play Christmas music.

4. Christmas movies. Starting Thanksgiving Day we order Christmas movies from the library and watch them throughout the holiday season. Some of our favorites are Jingle All the Way, White Christmas, Holiday Inn, Miracle on 34th Street, A Christmas Carol, A Christmas Story, Christmas with the Kranks, and It's a Wonderful Life.

5. Christmas shopping. When my children were little, each year my husband would take them Christmas shopping. They would purchase gifts for each other and for me. I would then take them out to get their father a gift. They looked forward to doing this and enjoyed choosing the presents and coming home and wrapping them. Now that they are older, the boys go out by themselves, but they still take a lot of pleasure in shopping for the gifts.

6. Special services. Because we are so active in ministry there are many things we are involved in at church that we look forward to each year. Some of these special services and events are the children's Christmas program, the lighting of the Advent candles, making up Christmas baskets for struggling families, and our Christmas Eve candlelight service.

7. Gingerbread house. Each year I buy a kit and let the kids decorate the house. The boys don't participate any more but my daughter, Emily, loves this.

8. Special meals. On Christmas Eve we always have platters of finger foods and sparkling cider. The whole family looks forward to this each year. Christmas morning is a special breakfast and then of course, the main meal. We usually pick an unusual meal for Christmas day. After Thanksgiving, we are ready for something different than turkey. Generally, we choose food from a particular country, and we make a meal that is unusual and tasty.

9. Gifts. On Christmas day we take turns opening a gift. This way we can enjoy what each person has gotten as well as making the day last longer. My children have done this since they were little. I never liked the idea of everyone ripping into their gifts at once. As they've gotten older, we've been able to stretch it out throughout the morning, taking a break about midway through.

10. Christmas letter. We started this a few years ago and each year we write a Christmas letter to the children. This is a personal letter letting them know how much we love them and the strengths we've seen in them over the past year.

Those are some of our traditions. Again, come up with your own. Find what works for you and your family and is meaningful. You will find that establishing a few traditions enhance the holidays greatly!

December 3
There is Hope

Psalm 119:49 ~ Remember your word to your servant, for you have given me hope.

Psalm 119:74 ~ May those who fear you rejoice when they see me, for I have put my hope in your word.

Psalm 119:81 ~ My soul faints with longing for your salvation, but I have put my hope in your word.

Psalm 119:114 ~ You are my refuge and my shield; I have put my hope in your word.

Psalm 119:147 ~ I rise before dawn and cry for help; I have put my hope in your word.

Psalm 119:43 ~ Do not snatch the word of truth from my mouth, for I have put my hope in your laws.

Ever since I was a child I have loved Christmas. As I matured in my walk with the Lord, I also grew to love all the symbolism involved in the Christmas story. I find that it enhances my understanding of Christ's coming as a human to save mankind.

One of the things that I especially enjoy is the lighting of the advent candles each year. Each one of the five candles of the advent wreath represents some aspect of Christ's coming. One of the candles that we light each year is the candle of hope.

As you look at these verses in Psalm 119, you will see that the reason the psalmist has hope is because he trusts the Word of God. He knows God is reliable. The Lord can be trusted.

As you read the Bible and understand what it says, you can have joy and hope as well. As you seek out His promises, the Lord will speak to you through His word. That is why it is so important to spend time reading it on a regular basis.

Do you find yourself feeling hopeless, like things will never change? Read His word. Do you feel depressed and down? Read His word. Do you feel overwhelmed and stressed out. Read His word.

The solution is right before us, yet so often that is the last thing that we do. We find many excuses why we can't do it. We are all busy, and even more so during the holidays. We have a million things to do, but in order to keep it together we must spend time with the Lord each day.

You won't find hope in family gatherings. You won't find it in following traditions or making the holidays an extravaganza. You won't find it in the busyness of the month. The only way to have hope this Christmas and all year long is to dig into the Word of the Lord. Find what He has to say about your situation.

Trust Him and you will find your hope. Open His Word and be rejuvenated today.

Is there a time each day that you could set apart for digging into God's Word? What do you need to change to keep that appointment with the Lord?

_____

_____

_____

_____

_____

_____

_____

_____

_____

_____

_____

_____

_____

_____

_____

_____

_____

_____

December 4

Good News

Isaiah 52:7 ~

**How beautiful on the mountains
are the feet of those who bring good news,
who proclaim peace,
who bring good tidings,
who proclaim salvation,
who say to Zion,**

"Your God reigns!"

Have you ever received good news? News that brought a smile to your face, made your heart leap for joy, and put a spring in your step? Everyone wants to receive that type of news.

As believers we are to be the messengers of good news to others; the news of God's peace and His salvation. It is so easy to forget this. We have a purpose here on earth as believers. We are to proclaim what the Lord has done for us to those who do not know Him. It is not something we are supposed to keep to ourselves and hide away. We have to pass it on.

I love the mental picture of our feet carrying the news to all we meet. We have to go out to do this. We can't stay wrapped up in our own little world. Sharing involves going. Perhaps that means taking a hot meal to a shut-in. Maybe it means giving a ride to a neighbor or watching a friend's child when she needs a break. Perhaps, it is just listening to someone as they share their heartache. Sharing the good news involves activity and involvement in another person's life.

This time of the year, people may be particularly open to hearing this news. Christmas is the time of year when many feel depressed, stressed, and discouraged. This is the time that they especially need to hear of the love of Christ.

Remember to pass the peace of Christ to those you meet and who do not know Him. That may be your neighbors, family, and friends. Pass that peace on to all you come in contact with this week and in the months to come.

Be the one who brings the Good News to their lives. This news will bring lasting joy to them. And that is the best gift they can ever receive.

Who in your life needs to hear some Good News? How will you do that this week?

_____

_____

_____

_____

_____

_____

_____

_____

_____

_____

_____

_____

_____

December 5
A Taste of Heaven

Revelation 7:9-10 ~

After this I looked and there before me was a great multitude that no one could count, from every nation, tribe, people and language, standing before the throne and in front of the Lamb. They were wearing white robes and were holding palm branches in their hands. And they cried out in a loud voice: "Salvation belongs to our God, who sits on the throne and to the Lamb."

Have you ever reflected on what heaven will be like? My husband and I worked for ten years for an inner city ministry and attended a church that was multi-racial. There were times when everyone was lifting their voices in worship and I would receive a glimpse of what heaven will be like.

Christ's coming brought hope to the world. It makes my heart sing to think that Jesus is the culmination of thousands of years of people hoping for the Messiah. But the thing that is so exciting to me is that He didn't just come to bring hope to the Jews, or to Americans, or to Africans or Chinese people. He came to bring hope to all ethnic groups in every country and from every walk of life.

It is awesome to think of people of every nationality looking to Him for their hope. We can get so hyper-focused on ourselves and our own little communities and country, that we forget there are people from other nations that are turning to Jesus.

Many believers, however, have stereotypes and prejudices against those who are different from them. They need to work hard at letting go of these sinful attitudes and thoughts. God loves the whole world, not just our corner of it. If you struggle with this, pray and ask God to forgive you and for His help in changing these thoughts.

Just as the Israelites looked forward to the coming Messiah, we can look forward to the day when Jesus will come back and we will all be together in heaven worshiping the Lord. I long and hope for that day to come soon.

What sinful attitudes do you have towards those who are different than you? What can you do to work on changing these thoughts?

_____

_____

_____

_____

_____

_____

_____

_____

_____

_____

_____

_____

_____

December 6
The Mark of Love

1 John 4:7-8 ~

Dear friends, let us love one another, for love comes from God. Everyone who loves has been born of God and knows God. Whoever does not love does not know God, because God is love.

Many ranchers place their brand upon their herds of cattle. This brand sets them apart and lets everyone know to whom the cattle belong. It is a mark that shows their identity.

Those of us who profess Christ as Lord of our lives have a brand on us too. It is a mark that sets us apart, and shows others who it is we follow. The mark of a true believer is love for one another. We cannot say that we know God and love Him if we cannot love other people.

Time spent in fellowship with God should cause us to reach out in love. As we work on our vertical relationship with the Lord, our horizontal relationships should be marked by love. All too often, it seems as if people who say they love God do not show much love to other people.

You cannot be in communion with the Author of love and not have love for your brothers and sisters in Christ. It is through our relationship with God that love for other people will grow.

I think it's appropriate during this Christmas season to remind ourselves of this. God sent His son because He loved us. He wants us to demonstrate that love by loving others in turn.

If you have anger and hatred in your heart towards another then it is time to look at your relationship with the Lord. Communion with God flows into sweet fellowship with others.

Let's look to the Lord of Love to help us learn to love those around us, even those who seem unlovable.

Is there someone in your life that you need to forgive? Do you have difficulty showing love to others? Pray and ask the Lord to help you with this.

_____

_____

_____

_____

_____

_____

_____

_____

_____

_____

_____

_____

_____

Christmas Morning Cinnamon Rolls

Ingredients:
2 cups warm water
2 pkg. Dry yeast
¼ c. sugar
1 ½ tsp. salt
1 egg
¼ c. margarine
6-6 ½ cup flour

Dissolve the yeast in the water. Add the sugar, salt, egg and margarine until well mixed and dissolved. Add flour until a soft dough forms.

Turn out on a floured surface and knead until smooth and elastic. Place dough in a greased bowl, cover and chill several hours (can do this overnight).

Divide dough in half and roll each piece of dough to about 18x9".

Spread with softened or melted butter. Sprinkle brown sugar over the dough and then sprinkle a combination of cinnamon sugar. Roll up the dough like a jelly roll. Cut into 1 1/2" chunks and place on greased cookie sheet. Cover and let double in size.

Bake at 400 degrees for 15-20 minutes or until browned. Ice as desired.

Yield: Approximately 20 cinnamon buns

December 7
Are You Looking for Love in all the Wrong Places?

Isaiah 49:14-16 ~

"But Zion said, 'The Lord has forsaken me, the Lord has forgotten me.' Can a mother forget the baby at her breast and have no compassion on the child she has borne? Though she may forget, I will not forget you! See, I have engraved you on the palms of my hands; your walls are ever before me."

It is hard to find true love in this world. We long for someone to say, "I love you." We desire for someone to love us unconditionally. Yet, for most of us, there are so many lies ringing through our heads saying, "You are not good enough." "You are not smart enough." "You are worthless." "You are not wanted." "You are not loved."

Do you ever feel this way? Alone? Unimportant? Unaccepted and unloved? Are you, as the song says, "Looking for love in all the wrong places?" "Looking for love in too many faces?"

No one person will fulfill this need for love in our lives. People are sinful. They fail. They let us down, and they cannot give us what we need 100% of the time.

There is only one who can do this and that is the Lord. The Lord of the heavens loves each of you. He created you and lovingly molded you. He alone is sufficient for all your needs. People will disappoint you, but God never will.

I love the picture of God engraving our name on His hands. We are ever in His thoughts and He knows us intimately and cares about everything we go through. He knows our struggles and we can depend on Him even when we have no one else to depend on. He cares about every aspect of our lives, and we are worth something in His eyes. We are wanted, accepted, worthy and precious in His sight.

Throughout history God continually desired to have a relationship with man. Time and again, He reached out to His ultimate creation. Yet, man continuously turned from God and looked for love in all the wrong places and looked for love in too many faces. Finally, because He loved us so much, He came down to earth and dwelt among us to show us love in human form.

At Christmas, we picture Jesus as a baby. However, this is a very small part of the story. He grew from a baby to a man. He ministered to others, spent 33 years of His life with us and finally, was hung on a cross. As He was placed on that tree, His arms were spread wide in a symbolic embrace of the world for which He was dying.

If you look closely, you can see your name engraved on His hands in the form of nail prints.

How have you been looking for love in the wrong places? Turn those struggles over to Him and let Him work through them.

_____

_____

_____

_____

_____

_____

_____

_____

_____

_____

_____

_____

December 8
Spread Some Hope

Isaiah 9:2-7 ~

The people walking in darkness have seen a great light; on those living in the land of deep darkness a light has dawned.

You have enlarged the nation and increased their joy; they rejoice before you as people rejoice at the harvest, as warriors rejoice when dividing the plunder. For as in the day of Midian's defeat, you have shattered the yoke that burdens them, the bar across their shoulders, the rod of their oppressor.

Every warrior's boot used in battle and every garment rolled in blood will be destined for burning, will be fuel for the fire. For to us a child is born, to us a son is given, and the government will be on his shoulders. And he will be called **Wonderful Counselor, Mighty God, Everlasting Father, Prince of Peace.**

Of the greatness of His government and peace there will be no end. He will reign on David's throne and over his kingdom, establishing and upholding it with justice and righteousness from that time on and forever. The zeal of the LORD Almighty will accomplish this.

As we sat in the dark I could feel the depression start to settle over me. The electricity had been out for four days and as each day stretched on without heat, lights, or flushing toilets I felt more and more discouraged. Nights were the worst. All was dark and silent and without light there was not much I could do. At some point in the middle of the night on day four, the lights flickered and then came on.

23

In a split second, I felt hope and relief surge through me. The lights were on in the house and in my spirit.

Darkness, despair, depression and discouragement are what so many people live each and every day. They find it difficult to get out of bed in the morning. Christmas seems to bring these feelings out in people who are already struggling. Perhaps it is because they are reminded of what they may be missing. They begin to feel even more hopeless.

Yet, the Christmas message is about hope. It is about light shining in the darkness. The good news isn't just for Christmas. It is for all people each day of the year.

The Messiah, Christ Jesus, is the Hope of the World and I'm so glad that I have that hope in my life. That is hope for all people, no matter what their circumstances.

In turn, as believers, we are to spread that hope to others by living out the Good News through our words and actions. We are to help turn on the light in other people's lives.

As people look at your life, do they see the hope you have in Christ? Is there something about you that will point them to Jesus? As you live out your Christian walk, do you bring light to others?

As you go through the Christmas season and the year, make sure you are spreading the hope of Jesus by living your life for Him. **How has the Lord given you hope? Who can you share that with?**

_____

_____

_____

_____

_____

_____

_____

_____

_____

_____

_____

_____

_____

December 9
Strength in Weakness

Micah 5:1-4 ~

Marshal your troops now, city of troops, for a siege is laid against us. They will strike Israel's ruler on the cheek with a rod. "But you, Bethlehem Ephrathah, though you are small among the clans of Judah, out of you will come for me one who will be ruler over Israel, whose origins are from of old, from ancient times."

Therefore Israel will be abandoned until the time when she who is in labor bears a son, and the rest of his brothers return to join the Israelites.

He will stand and shepherd his flock in the strength of the LORD, in the majesty of the name of the LORD his God. And they will live securely, for then his greatness will reach to the ends of the earth. And he will be our peace.

"I feel so useless." A friend who struggles with a debilitating disease said this to me recently. She has a strong desire to do something with her life, yet has physical limitations. I encouraged her to begin to pray and see how God can use her, despite her weaknesses.

25

I reminded her that the few things she is able to do are not insignificant in God's eyes.

Bethlehem was a small, insignificant town and yet, was chosen to be the birth place of the Messiah. A baby born to poor, unimportant parents would be the Savior of the World.

God works best in things that are weak, insignificant and unimportant in the eyes of the world. I Corinthians 1:27 says *"God chose the weak things of the world to shame the strong. He chose the lowly things of this world and the despised things – and the things that are not – to nullify the things that are."*

God uses us in our insignificance. In our weakness we can see Him work. Through our insignificance and frailty, He is glorified and brings peace to humankind. When you feel the weakest is when God can use you the most.

That is wonderful news for us today.

Where do you feel weak? Pray and ask God to use you despite that weakness.

_____

_____

_____

_____

_____

_____

_____

_____

_____

_____

_____

_____

_____

Bizchochitos

Ingredients:
1 cup white granulated sugar
1 & 1/4 cup butter
1 large or extra large egg
1 & 1/2 teaspoon vanilla
1/8 cup brandy
3 teaspoons whole anise seed
3 cups all purpose flour - King Arthur is my favorite
1/2 teaspoon baking powder
1/2 teaspoon salt

For topping:
1 teaspoon cinnamon

Terri A. Groh

1/2 cup white granulated sugar

Preheat oven to 350 degrees

Cream together in a large mixing bowl: 1 cup white sugar, butter, egg, vanilla and brandy. Cream until mixture is light and fluffy. Mix in the anise seeds.
Mix together the flour, baking powder and salt in a small bowl. Add the flour mixture to the creamed sugar/butter mixture.

Dust a work surface or wooden board with flour. Divide the dough into three pieces. Roll the first piece to 1/4" thick. Cut the dough into desired shapes, using a cookie cutter.

Place the cookies on a parchment lined cookie sheet.

Mix the sugar and the cinnamon together. Sprinkle the mixture over the cookies on the tray. Bake cookies for 9 to 10 minutes or until they are firm and just browning around the edges.

Recipe makes about 6 to 7 dozen 2" to 3" cookies.

December 10
Be Still

Luke 2:4-7 ~

So Joseph also went up from the town of Nazareth in Galilee to Judea, to Bethlehem the town of David, because he belonged to the house and line of David. He went there to register with Mary, who was pledged to be married to him and was expecting a child. While they were there, the time came for the baby to be born, and she gave birth to her firstborn, a son. She wrapped him in cloths and placed him in a manger, because there was no guest room available for them.

Heaving body, cries of pain, tearing, and blood. Lungs desperately gasped as they filled with oxygen. Red face, and then cries rent the silence of the night. The birth of the Christ child was a momentous event in history that went unnoticed by many.

His birth would change the world. His coming would bring hope and life. Yet only a few rough shepherds came to see him. The rest of the world slept on, ignorant of this moment in time that would change the course of the world.

Today, we have peace because of His life. We have life because of his death. We have hope because of his resurrection.

Yet at this time of the year when we should stop and remember and acknowledge this wonder, we are so wrapped up in preparation. Preparing cookies that will be eaten and digested. Preparing gifts that will be tossed aside at some point and forgotten. Writing cards that will be thrown out and preparing for parties that will be over in a blink of an eye.

And Jesus, who is the reason we celebrate, is pushed back to some corner of our mind. Our Bibles lie unopened, collecting dust. Our attitudes and emotions wear thin because of our hurried lives.

Let's stop. Wait. Listen. Hear from God. Pause with wonder at that remarkable moment when the Savior of the World took on human form and made our joy possible.

It's in our stillness that we will find true peace.

What can you cut out or postpone so that you can be still long enough to hear from God?

_____

_____

_____

_____

_____

_____

_____

_____

_____

_____

_____

_____

_____

_____

_____

_____

_____

_____

_____

_____

December 11
Finding Peace

Isaiah 26:3-4 ~

You will keep in perfect peace all who trust in you, all whose thoughts are fixed on you! Trust in the Lord always, for the Lord God is the eternal Rock.

I have a vivid memory from a few years ago of walking in the woods as the snow gently fell around me. The air was crisp, and all was still. The only sound was that of my boots crunching through the new fallen snow. I had such a feeling of peace and comfort. There are so many times when I long for that feeling again.

How can you be at peace when things seem to be in turmoil all around you? How can you be peaceful when you have a to-do list a mile long and only so many hours in a day? What if your world is turned upside down? Or you are dealing with conflict on a daily basis? What about the times when things don't go the way you expect or desire? It can be difficult to find inner peace when your world is in chaos.

These verses in Isaiah certainly give us the answer to this. Remembering to keep our eyes fixed on the One who is our rock helps us to find that peace. Taking our thoughts off the circumstances and placing them firmly on the Lord and His promises is the key.

I love the image of God as a rock. The Lord is firm, sound, unmovable, solid - a boulder. Nothing shakes Him up. The things that we see as huge obstacles are nothing to Him. He can do all things and we only need to lay our fears, concerns and burdens at His feet.

As you learn to turn your cares over to Him and then concentrate on Him and His promises, you will have true inner peace. You will have peace knowing He is in control. Peace in the fact that He will handle things in His time. Peace in the promise that He has good things for your life. Peace in the knowledge that He sees the big picture.

Trust Him. Focus on Him. Fix your eyes on Him. He will bring you peace.

What things do you need to lay at the feet of Jesus today?

_____

_____

_____

_____

_____

_____

_____

_____

_____

_____

_____

_____

_____

December 12
Messy People

Matthew 1:1-17 ~

This is the genealogy of Jesus the Messiah the son of David, the son of Abraham:
Abraham was the father of Isaac,
Isaac the father of Jacob,
Jacob the father of Judah and his brothers,
Judah the father of Perez and Zerah, whose mother was Tamar,
Perez the father of Hezron,
Hezron the father of Ram,
Ram the father of Amminadab,
Amminadab the father of Nahshon,
Nahshon the father of Salmon,
Salmon the father of Boaz, whose mother was Rahab,
Boaz the father of Obed, whose mother was Ruth,

Obed the father of Jesse,
and Jesse the father of King David.

David was the father of Solomon, whose mother had been Uriah's
wife,
Solomon the father of Rehoboam,
Rehoboam the father of Abijah,
Abijah the father of Asa,
Asa the father of Jehoshaphat,
Jehoshaphat the father of Jehoram,
Jehoram the father of Uzziah,
Uzziah the father of Jotham,
Jotham the father of Ahaz,
Ahaz the father of Hezekiah,
Hezekiah the father of Manasseh,
Manasseh the father of Amon,
Amon the father of Josiah,
and Josiah the father of Jeconiah and his brothers at the time of
the exile to Babylon.

After the exile to Babylon:
Jeconiah was the father of Shealtiel,
Shealtiel the father of Zerubbabel,
Zerubbabel the father of Abihud,
Abihud the father of Eliakim,
Eliakim the father of Azor,
Azor the father of Zadok,
Zadok the father of Akim,
Akim the father of Elihud,
Elihud the father of Eleazar,
Eleazar the father of Matthan,
Matthan the father of Jacob,
and Jacob the father of Joseph, the husband of Mary, and Mary
was the mother of Jesus who is called the Messiah.

Thus there were fourteen generations in all from Abraham
to David, fourteen from David to the exile to Babylon, and
fourteen from the exile to the Messiah.

My grandmother has always been very interested in researching our family history. She has traced our family tree back to ancestors in England who came to America during the founding of this country. I find it interesting to see where I have come from, but don't share the same passion as my grandmother.

Genealogies are not that important to most people nowadays. However, in Jewish history they meant a great deal. It was the line of your house that showed your value in society. Your bloodline either brought you honor or disgrace.

I usually skip right over these in my reading because to be honest, I find them quite boring. However, as I read through the genealogy of Jesus, I find it interesting that five women are named. In a predominately male culture, this is fascinating in itself. However, there is something special about these women.

They are not special because they are respectable and wealthy women. No, they actually all have a questionable past.

Tamar was a Canaanite woman who tricked her father-in-law into sleeping with her so she would have a child and carry on the bloodline. Rahab was a prostitute. Ruth was a foreigner. Uriah's wife committed adultery with David. Mary was a teenage girl, pregnant by the Holy Spirit whom no one would have believed.

None of these women would have been held in very high esteem, yet they are mentioned in Jesus' genealogy. Jesus, who came to save the sick and the lost and outcast. He reached out to people with messy lives and his own bloodline is full of messy people. To me that is encouraging.

We don't have to have it all together and be respectable to come to Him. He takes us where we are. He works with us despite the mess. We don't have to be perfect, polished and poised. As He touches our lives, the mess gets cleaned up. We don't have to do it in our own strength and we don't have to wait to get it together before we can approach Him.

That is the good news of the Christmas message for us all.

Have you been feeling inadequate? Not good enough? Thank God that you are significant in His eyes. Praise Him for the fact that you don't have to be perfect to approach Him.

_____

_____

_____

_____

_____

_____

_____

_____

_____

_____

_____

Gingerbread Ornaments

Ingredients:

4 cups of Flour
1 cup salt
1/4 cup cinnamon
3 Tbsp. nutmeg
2 Tbsp. ground cloves
1 1/2 cup warm water.

Mix all the dry ingredients together. Add the water a bit at a time until the dough is clay consistency. I found that I needed a bit more water. Roll out to 1/2 inch thickness. Make sure you poke a hole in the top of each ornament before you bake them.

Bake at 300 degrees for 1 hour. They will puff up a bit.

Cool on wire racks and decorate as desired. Some of the things we have used throughout the years are glitter glue, stickers, paint and jewels.

December 13
Are You Willing?

Luke 1:26-38 ~

In the sixth month of Elizabeth's pregnancy, God sent the angel Gabriel to Nazareth, a town in Galilee, to a virgin pledged to be married to a man named Joseph, a descendant of David. The virgin's name was Mary. The angel went to her and said, "Greetings, you who are highly favored! The Lord is with you."

Mary was greatly troubled at his words and wondered what kind of greeting this might be. But the angel said to her, "Do not be afraid, Mary; you have found favor with God. You will conceive and give birth to a son, and you are to call him Jesus. He will be great and will be called the Son of the Most High. The Lord God will give him the throne of his father David, and he will reign over Jacob's descendants forever; his kingdom will never end."

"How will this be," Mary asked the angel, "since I am a virgin?"

The angel answered, "The Holy Spirit will come on you, and the power of the Most High will overshadow you. So the holy one to be born will be called the Son of God. Even Elizabeth your relative is going to have a child in her old age, and she who was said to be unable to conceive is in her sixth month. For no word from God will ever fail."

"I am the Lord's servant," Mary answered. "May your word to me be fulfilled." Then the angel left her.

Why was Mary chosen above all the women in her day to carry the Son of God? Was there something about her that was superhuman? Did she possess some innate spiritual perfection that prompted God to pick her? Is she someone that we should worship or revere?

I don't believe so. I think the primary reason that Mary was chosen was that she was willing. She didn't question the angel, other than asking, "How can this happen if I've not been with a man?" She accepted her circumstances as a gift from the hand of God. She did this without doubt, without hesitation, without wavering, and with thanksgiving.

Because she was chosen, her life became harder. She faced pointing fingers and whispered words about her purity. She risked stoning and death because of this gift. She gave birth surrounded by animals and not by family. Her child would not be her own. As he grew into a man he was scorned and despised and forsaken. The things you want for your child such as success and honor and praise would not happen. Then she watched men beat him, crucify him and then saw him die.

This is a woman who is called blessed. As the many things happened to her and to her son, the scripture says she "treasured these things and pondered them in her heart." There was a quality about Mary that we should all have. It is a quality that the Lord finds pleasing.

It is the desire to be a willing vessel in God's hands. It is the desire to accept not just good from His hand but unpleasantness. How many of us, as we face struggles and trials, wish God would take it away? How many of us complain and moan and rail against God when things aren't going as expected? How many fall away from the faith when tragedies hit?

There will be things that go wrong – some minor and some tragic. What will your response be? Will it be to wail and moan and turn away? Or will it be to trust and to accept and to say as Mary did, "May your word be fulfilled." Will it be to put the trial in God's hand and let him work out the details? Are you willing to see what He wants you to learn from it? Willing to learn, grow and increase in faith?

I think Mary was chosen not because she was any more spiritual than anyone else. But because she was willing to let God do with her what He wanted. As a result, a child was born. A son was given. A savior has come.

Can you imagine what God can do through you if you are willing to be used?

What have you been holding back from God? How can He use you today?

No Stranger to the Manger
by Daniel Groh

Sometimes truth is not on the road paved in gold with glittering lights at night, nor in a palace or a rich man's house.

Or behind huge wealthy stained glass doors, where power preachers roar, and are recorded ever more. And parishioners park in their nice cars and clothes all looking so smart, from Macy's, Penney's, and Nordstrom's, never ever Wal-Mart.

Sometimes truth is on the road no one goes down, where there are no lights, but ugly sites, decrepit homes and broken dreams, where kids play on broken glass streets, to the constant sound of police beats.

And where there is smell of urine on the stairs and people hiding behind doors with constant cares, and wretched children happy with their Christmas hoard from Wal-Mart or the thrift store.

And their church on Sunday is behind barbed wire fence in a store, with a broken glass window and no stained glass door, but a poor old nameless preacher amongst a very small crowd, whose message will never be heard for the big religious airwaves loud.

Yet, in God's eyes, they are no stranger to the original manger.

December 14
A Peaceful Life

Isaiah 9:6-7 ~

For to us a child is born, to us a son is given, and the government will be on his shoulders. And he will be called Wonderful Counselor, Mighty God, Everlasting Father, Prince of Peace. Of the greatness of his government and peace there will be no end. He will reign on David's throne and over his kingdom, establishing and upholding it with justice and righteousness from that time on and forever. The zeal of the LORD Almighty will accomplish this.

Isaiah 53:1-6 ~

Who has believed our message and to whom has the arm of the LORD been revealed? He grew up before him like a tender shoot, and like a root out of dry ground. He had no beauty or majesty to attract us to him, nothing in his appearance that we should desire him. He was despised and rejected by mankind, a man of suffering, and familiar with pain. Like one from whom people hide their faces he was despised, and we held him in low esteem.

Surely he took up our pain and bore our suffering, yet we considered him punished by God, stricken by him, and afflicted. But he was pierced for our transgressions, he was crushed for our iniquities; the punishment that brought us peace was on him, and by his wounds we are healed.

We all, like sheep, have gone astray, each of us has turned to our own way; and the LORD has laid on him the iniquity of us all.

The nation of Israel had been in turmoil for many hundreds of years when these words of prophecy came to them. They had been in captivity and wandered through the desert. They were in constant war with the nations around them, and experienced many trials.

They were longing for a king who would ride in and conquer the nations around them. They were looking for the warrior who

41

would finally bring them justice and wipe out their enemies. They wanted justice.

God did as He promised. He sent His son to bring peace, but it was not the peace the Israelites expected nor was it in the package they anticipated.

Jesus did not come like a warrior, riding into battle. He came in the middle of a still, dark night. He was unexpected, unknown, born to a poor couple from Nazareth, and in the midst of animal filth. He died in the same manner that he was born. He was despised, rejected, a poor carpenter, and crucified with criminals who were considered filth.

Yet, because of His life and His death, we can have peace. An internal peace that comes no matter what circumstance you find yourself in.

The dictionary defines peace as 1) A state of tranquility or quiet; 2) freedom from disquieting or oppressive thoughts or emotions 3) harmony in personal relations 4) a state or period of mutual concord between governments

I find it interesting that the first two definitions of peace are concerned with internal peace rather than being at peace with those around us. It's almost impossible to have peace in our personal relationships, if we haven't made peace with God and we don't trust Him in all things.

Do you find yourself in a constant state of anxiety? Feeling worried? At war with yourself and those around you? Longing for peace?

Jesus came to bring peace; a peace that you can have even in the midst of difficult circumstances. You can have peace that can get you through any difficulty. He will give a peace that passes all human understanding. Your circumstances may not change, but your attitude towards them can.

When you put your faith in God, and daily walk with Him, you can have peace that calms your soul, and brings tranquility to your life. Make peace with God and you will have peace with others.

Do you have peace with God? Is there someone in your life you also need to make peace with? Ask the Lord to help you.

December 15
Sometimes We Just Need Some Encouragement

Luke 1:26-56 ~

In the sixth month of Elizabeth's pregnancy, God sent the angel Gabriel to Nazareth, a town in Galilee, to a virgin pledged to be married to a man named Joseph, a descendant of David. The virgin's name was Mary. The angel went to her and said, "Greetings, you who are highly favored! The Lord is with you."

Mary was greatly troubled at his words and wondered what kind of greeting this might be. But the angel said to her, "Do not be afraid, Mary; you have found favor with God. You will conceive and give birth to a son, and you are to call him Jesus. He will be great and will be called the Son of the Most High. The Lord God will give him the throne of his father David, and he will reign over Jacob's descendants forever; his kingdom will never end."

"How will this be," Mary asked the angel, "since I am a virgin?"

The angel answered, "The Holy Spirit will come on you, and the power of the Most High will overshadow you. So the holy one to be born will be called the Son of God. Even Elizabeth your relative is going to have a child in her old age, and she who was said to be unable to conceive is in her sixth month. For no word from God will ever fail."

"I am the Lord's servant," Mary answered. "May your word to me be fulfilled." Then the angel left her.

At that time Mary got ready and hurried to a town in the hill country of Judea, where she entered Zechariah's home and greeted Elizabeth. When Elizabeth heard Mary's greeting, the baby leaped in her womb, and Elizabeth was filled with the Holy Spirit. In a loud voice she exclaimed: "Blessed are you among women, and blessed is the child you will bear! But why am I so favored, that the mother of my Lord should come to me? As soon as the sound of your greeting reached my ears, the baby in my womb leaped for joy. Blessed is she who has believed that the Lord would fulfill his promises to her!"

And Mary said:

"My soul glorifies the Lord
 and my spirit rejoices in God my Savior,
for he has been mindful
 of the humble state of his servant.
From now on all generations will call me blessed,
 for the Mighty One has done great things for me—
 holy is his name.
His mercy extends to those who fear him,
 from generation to generation.
He has performed mighty deeds with his arm;
 he has scattered those who are proud in their inmost thoughts.

He has brought down rulers from their thrones
    but has lifted up the humble.
He has filled the hungry with good things
    but has sent the rich away empty.
He has helped his servant Israel,
    remembering to be merciful
to Abraham and his descendants forever,
    just as he promised our ancestors."

Mary stayed with Elizabeth for about three months and then returned home.

Confusion, anxiety, and fear may have gripped Mary's heart as she heard the angel's proclamation that she was pregnant. What would Joseph say? What would her parents say? What would her neighbors think? In a day and age where an unwed mother could be stoned, this was anything but good news.

After receiving the news, Mary got up and raced to Elizabeth's home. The first words out of Elizabeth were one of joy and excitement over the child in Mary's womb. It's no wonder that Mary's next response is to break into a song of praise to the Lord.

This young, teenage girl wanted to hear was that it was going to be alright. That is exactly what she heard from Elizabeth. Words of encouragement and acceptance came from this dear woman. They were words that caused Mary's heart to leap with joy.

Isn't that true in our own lives? When we are carrying a burden, often what we want to hear from others is that it's going to be okay. We want to feel love, acceptance and encouragement from other people. We want to know that even though we can't see the end result, God's plan is good and it will be alright.

Do you make sure that you encourage others in the same way you want to be encouraged? Do you speak words of affirmation and love to those around you? Do you reassure those going through difficult times that it will be okay?

Just as Elizabeth caused Mary's heart to sing, make sure that you do the same. Speak words of joy and excitement to others. Speak words of encouragement. Just give a hug when a hug is needed.

Mary stayed in Elizabeth's home for three months. It was a safe place for her. It was a home where she felt loved and cared for and accepted. Make sure that you are doing the same to those around you.

Who can you encourage today?

_____

_____

_____

_____

_____

_____

_____

_____

_____

_____

_____

Cinnamon Pinwheels

Ingredients:
2 cups flour
1/2 tsp. Baking powder
1/4 tsp. Salt
1/4 cup red hot cinnamon candies
3/4 cup butter
3/4 cup sugar
1 large egg
1/2 tsp. vanilla

Combine flour, baking powder and salt in a bowl.

In a mini food processor with a knife blade attachment (or coffee grinder), pulse cinnamon candies until finely ground.

In a large bowl or mixer, beat butter and sugar until smooth. Add egg and vanilla extract and beat on low. Gradually beat in flour mixture until just blended, occasionally scraping bowl with rubber spatula.

Transfer half of dough to a small bowl. Add the candy powder to the remaining dough and mix until well blended.

Between two 20-inch sheets of waxed paper, roll cinnamon dough into 15" x 10" rectangle. (If paper wrinkles during rolling, peel it off, then replace it to remove wrinkles). Repeat with plain dough.

Refrigerate dough 10 minutes or until chilled but still pliable. (I put mine on a flat tray to keep it from bending.)

Remove top sheet of waxed paper from each rectangle. Place plain rectangle (still on waxed paper) on work surface with long side facing you. Invert cinnamon rectangle on top of the plain rectangle so that the edges line up evenly.

Starting from a long side, tightly roll rectangles together jelly roll fashion, lifting bottom sheet of waxed paper as you roll.

Wrap log in waxed paper and freeze at least 1 hour or overnight, or until dough is firm enough to slice.

Slice into 1/4 inch thick slices and place slices 1 inch apart on a greased cookie sheet.

Bake in a 325 degree oven for 10-12 minutes or until lightly browned on the edges. Transfer to a wire rack to cool. Store cookies in tightly covered container at room temperature up to 1 week or in freezer up to 3 months.

December 16
Cover Your Mouth

Luke 1:5-20 ~

In the time of Herod king of Judea there was a priest named Zechariah, who belonged to the priestly division of Abijah; his wife Elizabeth was also a descendent of Aaron. Both of them were upright in the sight of God, observing all the Lord's commandments and regulations blamelessly. But they had no children, because Elizabeth was barren; and they were both well along in years.

Once when Zechariah's division was on duty and he was serving as a priest before God, he was chosen by lot, according to the custom of the priesthood, to go into the temple of the Lord and burn incense. And when the time for the burning of the incense came, all the assembled worshipers were praying outside.

Then an angel of the Lord appeared to him, standing at the right side of the altar of incense. When Zechariah saw him, he was startled and gripped with fear. But the angel said to him, "Do not be afraid, Zechariah; your prayer has been heard. Your wife wife Elizabeth will bear you a son, and you will give him the name, John. He will be a joy and delight to you, and many will rejoice because of his birth, for he will be great in the sight of the Lord. He is never to take wine or other fermented drink, and he will be filled with the Holy Spirit, even from birth. Many of the people of Israel will he bring back to the Lord their God And he will go on before the Lord, in the spirit and power of Elijah, to turn the hearts of the fathers to their children and the disobedient to the wisdom of the righteous – to make ready a people prepared for the Lord."

Zechariah asked the angel, "How can I be sure of this? I am an old man and my wife is well along in years?"

The angel answered, "I am Gabriel. I stand in the presence of God, and I have been sent to speak to you and tell you this good news. And now you will be silent and unable to speak until the day this happens, because you did not believe my words, which will come true at their proper time."

As a child I had a teacher that often had difficulty getting us to stop talking at the beginning of the class. Whenever we were talking and wouldn't listen, she made a signal for us to put one hand over our mouth and the other up the air. Once the entire class was quiet and ready in this way, she could begin to teach. Overall, it was an effective way to get our attention.

Zechariah, an upright man, was a priest in the temple of the Lord. One day as he takes his turn in the temple, and is lighting the incense, an angel appears to him with wonderful news. His wife, Elizabeth, whom had been barren for years, was to give birth to a child. This would not be an average child. He would grow and be the prophet, John, who would prepare the people to receive the coming Messiah.

49

Zechariah, who should have known better, immediately expresses disbelief. He asks, "How can I be sure of this?" "After all, my wife and I are old." He has the audacity to question God. An angel of the Lord is standing in front of him and giving him this great news and he expresses doubt.

The angel gives him a very succinct answer. "I am Gabriel." "I stand in the presence of the Lord and have been sent to tell you this good news." And then he doles out punishment because of Zechariah's doubt. He will be unable to speak until the child is born. It's as if God said, "You want to argue with me?" "I'm closing your mouth so you can't say anything!"

So many times we hear God speaking to us and He either directs us to follow Him or gives us some instruction. Yet, like Zechariah, we begin to express doubt and argue with God. We tell Him all the reasons it can't or won't happen.

Be careful that as you hear from the Lord that you don't become full of skepticism and disbelief at what He is telling you. Make sure you are not arguing with Him and expressing doubt about what God can do. Don't put Him in the position where He has to clamp His hand over your mouth.

How has God been speaking to you recently? Are you arguing with Him?

_____

_____

_____

_____

_____

_____

_____

_____

_____

_____

_____

_____

_____

Connections

Advent is one of my favorite times of the year. The word advent means coming; the coming of Jesus. Are you ready?

We seem to lose focus on why we celebrate very quickly. We get caught up in activities and busyness and while they are all good and nice, they do detract from the true meaning of our celebration.

There is so much symbolism in the birth of Christ, but there are also connections between his birth and his death. Here are some connections that I have found:

1. Some scholars believe that Jesus was actually born in a cave. It is interesting that neither of the two birth passages in Matthew & Luke mention the word stable at all. Many people in that day kept their

animals in naturally occurring outcroppings or caves. At the end of his life, Jesus was buried in a tomb. The tomb was actually a cave with a rock rolled in front of it. Both His birth and His death have the same humble beginnings.

2. The manger, an animal's feeding trough, would have been made out of raw, rough wood. It was not polished and pretty. The cross on which he hung was also raw, rough wood that was hammered together. No polish, no jewels, and no gold.

3. After Jesus' birth, He was laid in the manger. After His death, He was laid in the tomb.

4. Mary wrapped Jesus in cloths at His birth. Jesus' body was again wrapped in cloths at His death.

5. A handful of people witnessed the miracle of His birth. A handful of people witnessed evidence of the miracle of His resurrection.

6. A star, shining brightly in the sky lit the way for Jesus birth. The light of sunrise lit the reality of His resurrection.

7. Jesus breathed His first breath of life with the tearing of his mother's body. He breathed His last breath of life with the tearing of the temple curtain.

8. Both the place of His birth and the place He was buried were borrowed. Poverty was the mark of His birth and death.

There are so many wonderful connections in the birth and death of Christ. It's easy to miss them when we are racing around celebrating. We get so caught up in the preparation of Christmas that we forget to acknowledge His coming. We get caught up in pomp and circumstance and forget that He came in quiet and stillness.

Let's stop and reflect on why we have hope. Hope came into the world in the person of Jesus Christ. Don't forget that in all the preparation. Don't forget that as soon as Christmas is over.

Hope lives in our hearts year round because we worship the Lord of the Universe.

December 17
Fill up on Bread

John 6:51 ~

I am the living bread that came down from heaven. Whoever eats this bread will live forever. This bread is my flesh, which I will give for the life of the world."

I sold bread at a local farmer's market one year and I made over a hundred loaves of warm crusty goodness. I made so many loaves that I didn't need a recipe, and could almost make it with my eyes closed.

Bread is the most basic of food and adorns every table all over the world. For some it's used to fill in a meal and make it stretch and for others it may be the only meal they receive for days. It is inexpensive to make, filling, and for some, life giving. The loaf is kneaded to release the gluten which gives bread its fullness.

Jesus, born thousands of years ago, called Himself the bread of life. This one event in history, the birth of Christ, radiated life. The bread of life breathed the breath of life in a town whose name meant, "House of Bread." He was then laid on a bed of life giving hay.

Bread was a major theme throughout His life.

His first temptation in the desert was the temptation of bread or sustenance. Satan urged Him to use His power to feed Himself. Yet, He came to feed others. He came to give His life to others.

He called himself the Bread of Life. Jesus fed the five thousand with a few fish and small loaves of bread. He filled them up on physical bread and then immediately afterwards told His disciples that He was the bread that would satisfy. They were to fill up on Him.

He also told his disciples that there was a great harvest. He encouraged them to send workers out into the fields to harvest the crop and give them life. He encouraged them to give them bread, and to give them His message.

One of the final acts before His crucifixion was to break bread with His disciples. He fed them physically and then told them to continue to eat the bread after His death as a symbol of His body broken for them.

After the resurrection, one of the first acts Jesus did was to make a meal of fish and bread for His disciples. Immediately afterwards He tells Peter to feed His sheep. Feed His people the life giving bread that is Jesus and His message.

Jesus is the bread that satisfies. He fills you up and stays with you. Just as the kneading and yeast cause the bread to rise and become full, our lives are squeezed and kneaded so that as we follow Christ and trust Him, He gives us the fullness of life.

Bread, sustenance, life, Jesus. He came as bread. He came to give us sustenance. He died so we may have life. As we reflect on these things at Christmas, remember to take of the living bread. Christ didn't just come to earth as a baby. He developed into a man and ministered here on earth. He came to die for you. He conquered death through His resurrection.

Eat and remember Christ's body that was broken for you.

Have you accepted Christ as the living bread? Has He given you new life? Pray and ask Him to fill you with his life.

_____

_____

_____

_____

_____

_____

_____

_____

December 18
Turn on the Lights

Luke 2:8-20 ~

And there were shepherds living out in the fields nearby, keeping watch over their flocks at night. An angel of the Lord appeared to them, and the glory of the Lord shone around them, and they were terrified. But the angel said to them, "Do not be afraid. I bring you good news that will cause great joy for all the people. Today in the town of David a Savior has been born to you; he is the Messiah, the Lord. This will be a sign to you: You will find a baby wrapped in cloths and lying in a manger."

Suddenly a great company of the heavenly host appeared with the angel, praising God and saying,

"Glory to God in the highest heaven, and on earth peace to those on whom his favor rests."

When the angels had left them and gone into heaven, the shepherds said to one another, "Let's go to Bethlehem and see this thing that has happened, which the Lord has told us about."

So they hurried off and found Mary and Joseph, and the baby, who was lying in the manger. When they had seen him, they spread the word concerning what had been told them about this child, and all who heard it were amazed at what the shepherds said to them. But Mary treasured up all these things and pondered them in her heart. The shepherds returned, glorifying and praising God for all the things they had heard and seen, which were just as they had been told.

Matthew 2:1-4 ~

After Jesus was born in Bethlehem in Judea, during the time of King Herod, Magi from the east came to Jerusalem and asked, "Where is the one who has been born king of the Jews? We saw his star when it rose and have come to worship him."

Matthew 2:16-18 ~

When Herod realized that he had been outwitted by the Magi, he was furious, and he gave orders to kill all the boys in Bethlehem and its vicinity who were two years old and under, in accordance with the time he had learned from the Magi.

Then what was said through the prophet Jeremiah was fulfilled: "A voice is heard in Ramah, weeping and great mourning, Rachel weeping for her children   and refusing to be comforted,   because they are no more."

A group of dirty, poor shepherds taking care of the sheep one night see a wondrous sight. A fantastic light filled the sky. Angels appeared and brought incredible news. Their savior had been born. Joy filled their hearts. They believed. They came to worship.

Some intelligent, well-to-do wise men, pouring over their star charts see a wondrous sight. A fantastic new star filled the sky. Its light brought them incredible news. A savior had been born. Joy filled their hearts. They believed. They came to worship.

One shrewd, evil man, plotting his lordship hears of a wondrous event. Travelers from the east brought incredible news. A new King had been born. Dismay filled his heart. He believed. *He* wanted to be worshiped. And so he murdered innocent children.

As we consider joy this Christmas, I want to ask the following questions. How can we have joy when loved ones die of cancer? How can there be joy when we lose our jobs and struggle to make ends meet? How can we have joy when it's a struggle to get out of bed each morning? How can we experience joy when senseless violence takes the lives of men, women and children every day?

We can't have joy if we keep Jesus as a tiny baby in a manger. We won't have it if we keep him nailed to the cross or buried in the tomb.

The only way to experience true joy is if we acknowledge that He rose again. He rose with the light of dawn to give us joy. We experience joy in knowing that He is with us in the midst of this dark world.

The world itself doesn't become light because of His resurrection. We still experience hardship and persecution and tragedy. Senseless violence still happens. However, we have His light inside us, guiding us through the darkness.

We can have joy because He can turn our trials and tragedies into a vessel to fill us with more of Him. He lights our path and helps us find our way through the tribulation. His light brings hope in the midst of despair.

We in turn, as believers of Jesus Christ, can turn on His light to a very dark world. We can shine hope and peace in the darkness. We can bring light to our neighbors, co-workers and community in the midst of the blackness of night.

We can do this because His light fills us with the ability to have joy as we rely and trust Him to guide us through the darkness. We have joy as we focus on bringing comfort, love and help to those struggling. We have joy as we rely on Him to work through our circumstances to bring about His glory.

Joy is possible this Christmas because of the light He brings.

Is there someone in your life to whom you can bring comfort, love and help? What tangible ways can you do that this Christmas?

_____

_____

_____

_____

December 19
Special Messengers for a Special Event

Read Luke 2:8-14 ~

And there were shepherds living out in the fields nearby, keeping watch over their flocks at night. An angel of the Lord appeared to them, and the glory of the Lord shone around them, and they were terrified. But the angel said to them, "Do not be afraid. I bring you good news that will cause great joy for all the people. Today in the town of David a Savior has been born to you; he is the Messiah, the Lord. This will be a sign to you: You will find a baby wrapped in cloths and lying in a manger."

Suddenly a great company of the heavenly host appeared with the angel, praising God and saying, "Glory to God in the highest heaven, and on earth peace to those on whom his favor rests."

I loved making snow angels as a child. I would lie in the snow and wave my arms and legs and then try to get up without disturbing the image. In fact, I believed that if I got up without ruining it, an angel would watch over me.

People are obsessed with angels nowadays. They talk about guardian angels, angels of mercy, and sightings of angels. Yet, very little is said about them in the Bible.

Angels are only mentioned a few times in the scriptures. These "messengers" of God were sent to intervene or bring God's message of love.

An angel appeared to Zechariah to tell him of Elizabeth's pregnancy. An angel appeared to Mary to let her know she was the chosen one. An angel appeared to Joseph in a dream to beseech him to take Mary as his wife and not divorce her.

The angels heralded the news of Christ's birth to the shepherds. An angel warned the Magi in a dream not to return to Herod. An angel warned Joseph in a dream to go to Egypt to escape Herod's wrath.

It seems as if this one event in history was such a special occasion that the Lord sent his messengers to make sure that nothing would go wrong. His ultimate love for us in the birth and death of His son was something He desired enough to send these servants of His to intervene in human affairs.

Each of these times, the angel pointed people to God. Their job was to direct people to the source of all creation. Angels are special messengers, used by God, but they were never meant to be worshiped. Let's remember to worship the source and not the messenger. The message they gave, brought joy to all who heard it.

Take some time today and thank God for the wonderful message that the angels brought!

_____

_____

_____

Terri A. Groh

_____

_____

_____

_____

_____

_____

_____

_____

_____

_____

The Christmas Surprise

We were so blessed one Christmas because of a special gift we planned for my husband. The best part of this story is that God taught me a lesson and my children learned how God provides.

Dan had been working on a used laptop for years and it finally died on him one day. Because we had no money to purchase a new one, he spent months hand writing his sermons and then trying to squeeze in time on the family computer to type them there.

We wanted to get him a laptop but honestly didn't think it would happen because we were so tight financially. However, the boys and I started trying to pool our money to make this happen.

I saved every bit of extra money I made through sewing or baking. Generally, I only make $10-$20 here or there so it was going to take a long time to save for this. The boys both chipped in their share of the money and after a few months we had a significant amount saved to get the gift.

One day, we learned of a family in need of financial help. They were in a very hard spot and I began to feel the Holy Spirit nudging me to give them the money I had saved. I finally spoke with Dan about it and told him we had money saved for a gift for him without telling him what we had planned. He immediately said, "I don't need a gift." "Let's give it to them." The boys were in agreement and so we gave the money to this family.

I have to be honest and say that I struggled. I'm embarrassed to say I cried a bit too. Not because I didn't want to help someone else out, but because I really wanted to give my husband a nice present. He usually gets homemade gifts, as well as small items such as coffee, t-shirts, or socks. He works so hard and never asks for anything. He would rather help someone else out then get a gift himself.

However, I worked through my emotions and felt at peace about it. I resigned myself to giving him socks or coffee or something small once again.

Then all of the sudden, I started getting an unexpected order here or there. The money started to add back up a bit, though not even close to what I had before. However, within four days, I received three anonymous gifts in the mail, equaling the exact amount we gave away, and exactly the amount needed for Dan's gift. We even had money left over for our Christmas dinner.

God is awesome! I'm not saying that just because you give money away you'll get it back. I don't believe that. Sometimes God wants us to give generously just because that's what we should do. But I was thrilled that He did give it back and we were able to give Dan a wonderful Christmas present that year.

December 20
A Reason for Hope

Psalm 43 ~

Vindicate me, O God,
and plead my cause against an ungodly nation;
rescue me from deceitful and wicked men.

You are God my stronghold.
Why have you rejected me?

Why must I go about mourning,
oppressed by the enemy?

Send forth your light and your truth,
let them guide me;
let them bring me to your holy mountain,
to the place where you dwell.

 Then will I go to the altar of God,
to God, my joy and my delight.
I will praise you with the harp,
O God, my God.

Why are you downcast, O my soul?
Why so disturbed within me?
Put your hope in God,
for I will yet praise him,
my Savior and my God.

So many people begin to get the blues at this time of the year. Even though most Christians don't like to admit that they get down, they too can fall into this. We set up false expectations. We want our Christmas to be picture perfect and everyone to have warm fuzzy feelings. When reality doesn't meet our expectations, we feel discouraged.

Even David had times of discouragement and despair. He often felt like God had rejected him and left him at the mercy of his enemies. However, after complaining in this particular Psalm, David goes on to praise the Lord. In the last verse he gives himself a little lecture. He asks himself, "Why are you so depressed?" "Put your hope in God and it will turn out okay."

I know for me the solution to feeling down and depressed is to focus on what God is doing in my life. I try to remember the hope that I have and to offer praise to Him. When I do these things, my whole outlook on life begins to change.

Are you feeling overwhelmed, discouraged and ready to give up? Remember the hope that you have. Remember what the Lord has done for you. Put your hope in Him and give Him praise today!

List some things that God has done for you over the past week.

Terri A. Groh

Christmas Meringues

Do not double this recipe. You will need to make one batch at a time, washing the bowl/beaters between each batch.

Ingredients:

2 egg whites
1/8 tsp. cream of tartar
1/8 tsp. salt
3/4 c. white sugar
6 ounces of chocolate chips
1/2 c. crushed peppermint candy (I used a coffee grinder to grind the candy up into almost powder and it took 14 round peppermint candies to make 1/2 cup of powder)
1/2 tsp. vanilla

Preheat oven to 300 degrees.

Beat egg whites until frothy. Add cream of tartar and salt. Beat until stiff and peaks form. (It's important that the egg whites are stiff). Add sugar gradually, beating constantly.

Fold in chocolate chips, candy, and vanilla.

Drop by teaspoonful on cookie sheets lined with parchment paper.

Bake for 20 minutes or so, until the cookies look baked. Do not brown. Remove from paper when cool. They freeze well.

December 21
He Knows

Psalm 56:8-11 ~

You keep track of all my sorrows.
You have collected all my tears in your bottle.
You have recorded each one in your book.

My enemies will retreat when I call to you for help.
This I know: God is on my side!
I praise God for what he has promised;
Yes, I praise the Lord for what he has promised.
** I trust in God, so why should I be afraid?**
What can mere mortals do to me?

There have been times in my life when I have felt so utterly alone in the midst of tremendous grief. It seemed as if no one cared and even the Lord seemed to have deserted me.

I love these verses in Psalm 56. God does see our sorrows. He knows our heartbreaks and disappointments. He keeps a record of our hurts. They do not go unnoticed by the Lord. He holds them in His hands.

What a wonderful thought. We are not alone in our struggles. The Lord is on our side and takes our cares and concerns on His shoulders. He walks with us through our trials.

So often, I feel fearful about a situation and yet, these verses tell me that the God of the universe is watching out for me. There is absolutely nothing that anyone can do to us that will change the fact that God will do what He promised in our life.

The focus during the Christmas season is on joy. There is great joy in knowing that the Lord sees my hurt and lifts me up and helps me through the hurdles. He also remembers the pain and struggle involved in my trial, and continues to comfort me and help long after the situation is over.

Your tears do not fall unnoticed. You are not alone. You are loved. That should bring you great encouragement and joy. God is with you today in the midst of your struggle.

Are you struggling with something now? Give it to the Lord. Let Him carry that burden.

December 22
Extravagant Love

I John 3:1 ~

How great is the love the Father has lavished on us, that we should be called children of God! And that is what we are!

As a child, I would pour over the Sears and Roebuck Catalog. I loved looking at the pages and pages of toys. I would dream of having anything I wanted from that book. I also loved looking at the Christmas pages and the huge trees loaded with gifts and ornaments. I imagined having parents that would give me presents like that.

As an adult, one of the things I love about Christmas is that I'm reminded over and over again of the extravagant love of our Heavenly Father. He has lavished us with the greatest gift ever given.

He loved us so much that He gave up His most precious possession, His son. He gave up His child so that we could be adopted as His children. What a wonderful thought that is for us.

Because of this extravagant love, we in turn should be lavish in our love towards others. That love should pour out of us and touch all we come across. Extravagant love goes above and beyond the normal. It is generous. It is sacrificial. It is selfless.

How are you showing that love towards others today? Are you withholding love because it's inconvenient? Do you hold back because you don't feel like it? Or because you have your own desires you would rather work on?

As we go through this Christmas week, let's reflect on how we can be lavish in the love we show others. Let's not be stingy with our love. Instead, let's be known as extravagant people.

Is there someone you have been withholding love from? How can you change that?

_____

_____

_____

_____

_____

_____

_____

_____

_____

_____

_____

_____

December 23
Anonymity

Matthew 11:4-6 ~

Jesus replied, "Go back and report to John what you hear and see: The blind receive sight, the lame walk, those who have leprosy are cleansed, the deaf hear, the dead are raised, and the good news is proclaimed to the poor. Blessed is anyone who does not stumble on account of me."

Silver bells. Christmas lights twinkling. Wreathes. Carols. Shopping. Glitz, glamour and glimmer. These are all things we associate with Christmas. Yet Jesus came in stillness, anonymity, and poverty. His birth wasn't glamorous. There was no pomp and circumstance associated with it. No wealth. No hoopla.

Christ came into the world as a baby born to simple parents. Mary and Joseph were poor, powerless and oppressed. Parents like many in the world. Perhaps, parents like you and me.

Could Jesus have chosen to be born in a palace? Yes. Could He have been born into a wealthy family? Absolutely. But He didn't.

He came in poverty and hopelessness and hardship. Yet, His life brought hope. He brought peace. He brought joy and He brought love. His birth provided hope to the hopeless. Peace to the powerless. Joy to the joyless and love to the unlovely and unloved. And He still does that today.

That is the good news of the Christmas story. That is the reason we celebrate Christmas. That is what this season is about. *Not the trappings. Not the activity. Not the presents.*

Christ came to bring hope. He came in poverty so that both the affluent and the impoverished can know the hope that He brings. God became nobody so that everybody could become somebody.

How has he brought you hope, and peace, and love?

_____

_____

_____

_____

_____

_____

_____

_____

_____

_____

_____

_____

'Twas the Day Before Christmas

Twas the day before Christmas and all through the house Not a creature was stirring, not even a mouse... except Mom, who can't sleep and has a thousand things to do before the clock strikes seven for the Christmas Eve service at church.

It was 3 a.m. and I couldn't sleep so I finally decided to get up for a while instead of lying there tossing and turning. In the midst of my restlessness, I was also thinking about how easy it is to get caught up in activity and totally miss the meaning behind what we are doing. This is my biggest weakness. I rush around, do, work, prepare, but do very little enjoying the moment.

71

Terri A. Groh

I want to spend time with my family and enjoy them. I don't want to spend my days racing around, screeching like a maniac, "Get out of the way, I have things to do."

Does it matter if there is only one kind of Christmas cookie this year? Will anyone notice if the bread is from the store and not homemade? Will my family care if the house is messy when we open gifts on Christmas Day?

I have to keep reminding myself that making memories is more about the feelings invoked in remembering, not all the things that were done. When I think of my fondest memories growing up, almost without fail, they have to do with *relationship* and not things or activities.

So on this eve of Christmas, I am going to slow down, enjoy, feel, think, and experience. I'm going to look my husband and children in the eye, listen to them with my whole self engaged, and laugh and love. I'm going to fight down the urge to have everything just "so." I'm going to quell the feeling that I have to do just *one more thing*.

I'm going to find true meaning in the wonderful gift God gave so many years ago. I think the greatest gift I can give my family this year is the gift of me, fully engaged and available.

That is my prayer for me and that is my prayer for you too. Have a very "slow down and enjoy the moment" Merry Christmas.

December 24
Love with Skin

I Thessalonians 5:11 ~

Therefore encourage one another and build each other up, just as in fact you are doing.

As I sat crying after going through a traumatic moment one day, a friend came and sat beside me and rubbed my back. She didn't say anything, but just kept moving her hand in circles. Her warm touch showed me how much she loved and cared for me. She didn't give me pat answers. She didn't spout off platitudes. She showed me her love through her touch.

So many times when we go through difficulties, people offer to pray for us. Those prayers and words of encouragement are so precious. However, the thing that seems to help the most and really lift our spirits is someone who is willing to go out of their way to give a hug, to come and sit and visit, or to help in some physical way.

I think this is the heart of the Christmas message. God sent His son, Jesus, to earth so that we could touch, feel, and see His love in a very tangible way. Jesus was God's love with skin.

As we go through this Christmas week, it's easy to get caught up in our own preparations and get so hyper-focused on our families that we forget to show others God's love.

As you go through this week, look around you and see who is discouraged or hurting. Offer a helping hand to someone who needs it. Sit and offer words of encouragement to someone who is struggling. Help someone who perhaps is having a difficult time during this holiday season by giving a gift or two.

Remember that while your prayers and words of encouragement are vital, many people also need to physically see and feel God's love.

Be God's love with skin this Christmas.

What specific thing can you do today to show God's love?

_____

_____

_____

_____

_____

_____

_____

_____

_____

_____

_____

_____

December 25
A Reason for Celebration

Luke 2:11 ~

Today in the town of David a Savior has been born to you; he is the Messiah, the Lord.

This is it. The day we've been waiting for. The count-down to Christmas day is over and all the many weeks of preparation are finished. The gifts are purchased and wrapped, cookies have been made. Christmas movies are being watched, parties have been attended and Christmas music is playing.

However, have you spent the same amount of time preparing your heart? Are you spending time in God's word each day? Are you seeking the Lord in prayer? Are you asking Him to speak to your hearts during this time? Are you looking around to see if there is someone else you can bless?

Do you know that Christmas is one of the biggest stress producers? We are stressed with family relationships and expectations we put on ourselves or others put on us.

Somehow this seems so sad to me. We've made Christmas into this giant holiday frenzy that it never was meant to be. This should be a time when we are especially blessed at the wonder of Christ's coming to earth

As you enjoy the festivities today, please take time to stop and listen to what God wants to say. What is it He wants you to get out of this holiday? Stop the busyness for a time each day and just hear from the Lord.

Let's not forget the true reason we celebrate today. Let's work on being blessed and not stressed.

What thing does God want you to hear today? How can you reach out to another person today or this week?

_____

_____

_____

_____

_____

_____

_____

_____

_____

_____

_____

_____

December 26
Don't Take Your Gift for Granted

John 3:16 ~

"For God loved the world so much that he gave his one and only Son, so that everyone who believes in him will not perish but have eternal life."
I John 4:7-9 ~
"Dear friends, let us continue to love one another, for love comes from God. Anyone who loves is a child of God and knows God. But anyone who does not love does not know God, for God is love.

God showed how much he loved us by sending his one and only Son into the world so that we might have eternal life through him."

Would you give your child up in order to save another? How many would be willing to sacrifice a family member in order to save another life?

I feel overwhelmed at the wonder of the gift that God sent to us. I have eternal life because of the sacrifice of a son. He gave His child knowing that He would be spit upon. God knew His son would be mocked and rejected and killed. He did it knowing that through Jesus' death we would have a way to have a relationship with Him. There is nothing more precious to me than that thought.

Yet, so often, we run through our days and never think about it. We don't value it. We take it for granted. That is one of the wonderful things about holidays such as Christmas and Easter. They force us to slow down and reflect on this wonderful gift.

As you continue to enjoy the Christmas season, make sure you remember why you are celebrating. Take time to stop and thank Him for the blessings He has given to you. Don't take His gift for granted. Make sure you thank the Giver of all your blessings.

Then, as an outpouring of the love shown to you, make sure that you also are showing love to others. That is the true mark of being His child. When we realize the love that was shown to us, how can our response be anything less?

Take some time today to thank God for His precious gift. What specific things can you do today to show others this love?

_____

_____

_____

_____

_____

_____

_____

_____

_____

_____

_____

Candied Pecans

Ingredients:
2 cups pecan halves
1 cup sugar
1 tsp. cinnamon
2 tsp. vanilla extract
1/4 cup of water

Place all the ingredients in a stick proof skillet and cook over medium high, stirring constantly for 6-10 minutes.

The pecans will start to glaze and the liquid will evaporate. Remove from the pan and add 2 tsp. of water to steam the pecans. Stir to coat all of the pecans with the water. Place on parchment paper on a cookie sheet until cool.

Store in an airtight container.

December 27
Make Me a Servant

John 13:13-17 ~

"You call me 'Teacher' and 'Lord,' and rightly so, for that is what I am. Now that I, your Lord and Teacher, have washed your feet, you also should wash one another's feet. I have set you an example that you should do as I have done for you. Very truly I tell you, no servant is greater than his master, nor is a messenger greater than the one who sent him. Now that you know these things, you will be blessed if you do them."

For as long as I can remember, I have prayed that God would make me His servant. That I would do whatever it is He wanted me to do. That I would go wherever He wanted. I have prayed that I would point others to Him.

I feel like I have failed miserably in this endeavor, even though this is my desire. I get in the way. My flaws and sinful nature are constantly battling with the desire to serve Him. I fall prey to a variety of traps and slip into sin quite regularly.

One night I was complaining to my husband, Dan, about how there is so much to do and that we never get a day off. How everyone wants something from us and expects us to be there for them at the drop of a hat and yet, no one is ever there for us. No one thinks about the fact that we never get a day to just cease all activity. And I went on and on.

Then I heard that still, gentle voice of the Holy Spirit reminding me of my prayer, "Make me your servant." "Give me the desire to do Your Will." "Allow me to point others to you." He also reminded me that His son was sent to serve. Jesus was there for others. He pointed others to God. Then I had to ask for forgiveness.

Christmas is the time of the year when I am reminded of how much He gave up for me. He gave it so that I could have hope and experience His love. He came so that I can feel joy and be filled with His peace.

My continued prayer is that I will be His servant, and that I would continue to point others to Him. My prayer for each of you is that you would also be His servant and that your life would point others to the Lord.

What attitudes do you need to change in order to point others to Jesus?

_____

_____

_____

_____

_____

_____

_____

_____

_____

_____

_____

_____

December 28
Letting Go

Luke 2:19 ~

 But Mary treasured up all these things and pondered them in her heart.

Nothing seems to make me more anxious than the well-being of my children. I long for them to be successful, content, and joyful. I want good things for them. I want them to be well-liked and have friends. Many times I lie awake in tears as I pray for a difficult situation they are facing, or an unkindness that has been done to them.

Did Mary struggle with anxiety over her firstborn? As He grew and exhibited signs of being special, did she long for a "normal" life for Him? As Mary held that little baby in her arms, did she feel fear? She obviously knew from the start that His life would be different. Perhaps she wanted Him to grow, be successful, have friends and be loved.

Yet, Jesus was ridiculed, scorned, despised and hated. He was maligned and rejected. He was beaten and crucified. I can only imagine the worry and sorrow Mary must have had.

As she pondered the shepherds visit, the magi who brought gifts, and later, heard her young boy teaching men much older than Himself in the temple, what emotions were coursing through her? What did she think?

Mary had to release her child to God and to the world. She had to let go of her expectations and dreams.

We, too, need to let go of our expectations for our children. God has a unique plan for each of them and it may be different than your plan. Can you let go?

God allows things in our children's lives because it is part of His purpose for them. Sometimes, our desire to protect them and keep them from all unpleasantness and unhappiness can actually be a detriment to them.

In the hard times we grow. In the tough times we hope. In the lean times we are stretched. Release your child into God's hands. He has a plan.

Be there for them, comfort them, and hug them. But don't try to fix every hard situation. Don't try to intervene in every problem.

Help them to develop a healthy prayer life and teach them to go to God with their problems and seek His will.

This Christmas season, take some time and ponder these things.

Ask the Lord to show you how you may be hindering His plan for your child.

_____

_____

_____

_____

_____

_____

_____

_____

_____

_____

_____

December 29
What is Required?

Micah 6:8

He has shown you, O mortal, what is good.
And what does the LORD require of you?
To act justly and to love mercy
and to walk humbly with your God.

A new year is right around the corner. I love January because it's like wiping the slate clean and having a fresh new start. It is the ultimate "do-over." It gives you the opportunity to set new goals and to think about what you would like to do differently in the coming year.

However, as you set out your goals or resolutions for the New Year, are you praying and asking the Lord what He would want from you? Are you seeking His will for your life? Are you hearing from Him and willing to make changes that He is setting before you?

I love this verse in Micah. What is it that the Lord requires from His people? This verse sums it up nicely in three things.

1. Act Justly - make sure that you are upright and honest in all your dealings. God is a God of justice. He expects His people to be the same. Treat those around you with dignity and respect. Cheating, lying, dishonest gain, disrespect of others is not something that should be characteristic of God's people.

2. Love Mercy - are you a merciful person? Do you exact revenge on those who hurt you? Do you run them down with your words? Are you quick to be offended and angry with others? Are you vindictive? We are to be people who forgive. We have been forgiven so much from the Lord. Let's make sure that we too are people who forgive others.

3. Walk Humbly With God - let's go through the New Year with the goal of walking with God in humility. So many people I know say they love the Lord and have a relationship with Him, yet they never read His word. They never seek Him out before they make a decision. They never worship with His people. They talk a good game, but the Lord requires more than speech.

Walking humbly with God means asking the Lord what He wants for your life. What direction He wants you to go. Seeking His counsel before you make a decision. Recognizing who is really in control of your life.

Seek out the Lord in the New Year. Ask Him for direction for your life. Make it your goal to walk in His ways in the coming year.

What is God requiring of you this year?

_____

_____

_____

_____

_____

_____

_____

_____

_____

_____

_____

_____

December 30
Keep the Proper Perspective

2 Corinthians 5:17 ~

"Therefore, if anyone is in Christ, he is a new creation; the old has gone, the new has come!"

Galatians 6:15 ~

"Neither circumcision, nor uncircumcision means anything; what counts is a new creation."

A new year is a wonderful time to look back over the previous months and see what you have accomplished and what needs to be changed. Many people love the feeling of a fresh start and looking forward and setting new goals for the coming year. It's a time of reflection, renewal and rejuvenation.

There are many scriptures that talk about being new. These verses are just a couple. When you decide to turn and follow the Lord, you become a new creation. Your former way of doing things - your thoughts, actions, and attitudes - all change.

How many times do we forget this though? How often do we run around and think it's the things that we *do* that count? In Galatians 6:15, Paul tells the church at Galatia that being circumcised or uncircumcised will not make a difference. What does matter is the change in their life brought about because they are following Christ.

What does this mean for us today? How many of us have a checklist of things that we set as the standard? How many think that going to church every Sunday is what counts? What about living a good, moral life? Being kind to our neighbors? Participating in community service?

These things are all important but they are meaningless if we have not committed our life to following Jesus Christ. They will not get you into heaven. They will not count for anything in God's eyes.

The only thing of importance is recognizing that we are nothing without the Lord. It is only by asking for His forgiveness and then following Him that we will find meaning. So often we act as if we will get into heaven through our good works. It's not what we *do* that matters, it is who we *are* in Christ. You don't have to do anything for God to love you and want a relationship with you.

So as we begin a new year, let's keep the proper perspective. It's not what you do, it's who you are.

Have you been trying to work your way into heaven? What things do you need to turn over to God?

_____

_____

_____

_____

_____

_____

_____

_____

_____

_____

_____

_____

December 31
Wipe the Slate Clean

Psalm 40:3 ~ He has put a <u>new</u> song in my mouth...

John 13:34 ~ A <u>new</u> commandment I give you, love one another

II Corinthians 5:17 ~ If anyone is in Christ, he is a <u>new</u> creation.

Ephesians 4:22-24 ~ ...put off your old self...be made <u>new in the attitude</u> of your minds...put on the <u>new self</u>, created to be like God in true righteousness and holiness.

I love cracking open a new book and seeing its crisp, clean pages. I enjoy opening a new journal or notebook and running my hand over untouched pages for the first time. I love the freshness of a brand new morning. The smoothness of fresh, clean sheets makes me sigh with contentment as I climb into bed.

These verses talk about this idea of newness. Tomorrow begins a brand new year. We have a fresh start and can wipe the slate clean and begin over.

God is the God of fresh starts. He has done a new work in our lives. He has given us a new beginning, and each day is a "do-over."

Because of what the Lord has done, we don't have to live out our old patterns and behaviors. He gives us the ability to change and grow and become like Him. He is doing something new and wonderful in us.

As we start a new year, praise God for fresh starts and the ability to begin again. I would encourage you to set some spiritual goals for yourself for the coming year and be self-disciplined to see those goals become a reality.

Aren't you glad that we have a God who wipes the slate clean?

Write out a prayer of praise, thanking God for a new start.

Terri A. Groh

Index of Biblical References

Old Testament

New Testament

ABOUT THE AUTHOR

Terri A. Groh has a B.A. in Psychology from Nyack College and also attended the Alliance Theological Seminary, working on her Master's of Divinity. She has been married to her husband, Dan for 25 years, and is mother to three children, Nathan, Stephen and Emily. She ministers alongside her ordained husband in a church about 70 miles north of New York City. She has a craft business, Terri's Country Crafts and Books, and loves to read, sew, cook, and write in her spare time. Terri writes a daily blog post at her website at www.terrigroh.com.

Made in the USA
Charleston, SC
11 September 2013